A Full C

MILES CHAMPION was born in Nottingham in 1968. He edited Tom Raworth's *As When* (Carcanet, 2015) and Ted Greenwald's *The Age of Reasons* (Wesleyan University Press, 2016), and, with Trevor Winkfield, co-authored *How I Became a Painter* (Pressed Wafer, 2014). He lives in Brooklyn, New York.

Also by Miles Champion from Carcanet Press

Compositional Bonbons Placate

Tom Raworth, *As When: A Selection* (ed.)

A FULL
CONE

Miles Champion

CARCANET

First published in Great Britain in 2018 by

Carcanet Press Limited
Alliance House, 30 Cross Street
Manchester M2 7AQ

Cover image: Rachel Harrison, *69, 2014 (detail);
wood, polystyrene, cement, acrylic, shopping cart, copper,
telephone, hula hoop, beer can and toy gun; 84 x 36 x 44 inches.
Courtesy the artist and Greene Naftali, New York.
Cover design: Diane Bertolo.

Printed in England by SRP Ltd.
A cip catalogue record for this book is available from
the British Library, ISBN 9781784104405.

The publisher acknowledges financial assistance
from Arts Council England.

for Larry, Ted and Tom

love always

ACKNOWLEDGEMENTS

Some of these poems were first published in *Sore Models* (Lowestoft, Suffolk: Sound & Language, 1995), *Compositional Bonbons Placate* (Manchester: Carcanet, 1996), *Facture* (Great Barrington, MA: The Figures, 1999), *Three Bell Zero* (New York: Roof, 2000) and *How to Laugh* (New York: Adventures in Poetry, 2014); and in *Arras*, *Critical Quarterly*, *The Delineator*, *Fell Swoop*, *Infinite Editions*, *PN Review*, *Talus* and *Tolling Elves*. 'Wet Flatware' and 'Air Ball' were written as furniture music for the accompanying drawings by Trevor Winkfield. Particular thanks to Diane Bertolo, Thomas Evans, Gustavo Gordillo and Rachel Harrison.

CONTENTS

A FULL CONE

FORENSIC ASPERITIES DOCKING

But unlike Gertrude Stein's rose, the stone is not a stone. The stone
Is a piece of paper

The glissade
Of why and how ... and eating-out of rust through
Meaning question.
                              arynoc c and b
we can't. Oh!—our unknown l.........e?"

—He and Mrs Throes (the widow)—
The numerals '3.18' written under the figure
Identify his initials as C. R. according to Whitman's
Schoolboy code.

TRANSCENDENTAL EXPRESS

The phrase 'ball of worsted'
                            is interesting
it is, indeed, a cupola
                            that dispenses with the material
revealed by the temptation to exist
                                    in the person of its author. But
if we linger a few moments
                            within its bounds
a retrospective *après coup*
                            (tongue)
or seeming irregularity
                            fills our heads with ideas
much more efficiently
                            and becomes more coherent, a thing.

The puzzle is
                    Why does the little girl hold
an orange
            in her hand?
Between 'orange' and 'worsted'
                                language
is both more real and more terrible.
                                    I do not intend to enter the field
where the pimpernel pellets
                            obtrude, nor will I
list, confirm
                this abundant practice. I
shall explore the innocuous sign
                                by methodical going.

In the Ukraine,
                on the Bug River
they sleep till summer
                        in an artichoke

which is longer and more detailed,
                           both literal and encoded.
The plastic character of grammar
                        seems to deride
the lexical excesses
                 of botany. Show us
                             how language constrains
a shed or a chair
                which claims to be nothing more than a
tchoki. Poetry
              can always be defeated
                           by a kind of
shuttle movement
                which threatens to subvert
                                but eventually upholds
its own laws. How do we
                     make the text blab
                                between 'worsted'
                        &
                     'orange'
           Do we
      extend recourse
                  to declension
beyond its actual
               (but contingent)
                        scope?
                  Beyond the sediments
                                that chatter
      I might not, if I could, yet I may. But I can
                              and still I must.

BLUE BAG

shops can also be
chips of foam.
tubular
you to lay threads.
or beans.
many of which are
chips of foam.

yarn, and a suggested
of needle and stitch to
reading ball.
three dots within.
work out from
never as
colours in same sequence on the scarf.
calculate how
of needle and stitch to
, armhole
of needle and stitch to
describe the placing
at random on yoke
reading ball.

or in blocks to
these are the most
commonly used
a medium hot oven
thick pulp.
lay strips
of objects into knitting
the most commonly
lay strips if necessary, remembering that
dense bead
on what you are seaming.

hot oven
the most commonly.

BEL AIR

Chef chef peignoir
While the women diamond drops
Now it's a cow
You broke it

And helio
Pall
Amid blown
Peacocks the vitality

Clasped
To lamented stop
The ability of the totemist
To be locked in the convulsions of a dance

Oleander perhaps or a larch
To mock the brooding moose
There is an empty
Pigeonhole waiting by her peplum

The biographer quite deranged
Neurasthenic and excitable
Flowers unguents
Pins and a big brown moon

Slips of the tongue or pen
Can still sometimes drug my senses
Another sign *mutton*
To go alongside *lamb*

Sheep when they are eaten
Have their ismatic side
Willy-nilly a structuralist nothing
Hearse coarse whores house horse

Nag mount pony steed
A Korean speaker
With the Jamjanets of course it was the *houla-houla*
Which survived in Czechoslovakia

Eating drinking and dressing
The existing cultural stock
Nineteen meringues
Made a charming toc-toc sound

Pursuing a rosy radish
Then finding Worcester Sauce
Colonel sweetish
Tarragon dashing *huile*

The ear suddenly allowed
Academic success I
Will obscure yet enhance
The beauty of a well-remembered stick

A sore thumb without
Apology without revisionism
Without the added
Colour sustained by peaches

A permanence of rain softens
The transition from pointillist
Gardeners in a fig
Held silently to resonate

Burn things and dream things
A Gin Daisy or a Brandy Flip
Blindness becomes sight
Nonsense

An idea
Its rheumatics

No sooner written than it starts
Overwhelming with intentions

Half a guinea for a comfit
If by denotation we mean a glance
The wind of language
Hoist by its own petard

Herd of the black hand
What the atlas tells us
No names no qualities
Receipt of the magic object

There is there syntax
Thrives on the repetitions
In botany
Strong men come out of the ring

I've a sprig of the real
Phrenology and cards and sand
Either speaker/writer or
Hearer/reader

A certain opacity for the writer
The cornucopia of the niggardly
Puzzles stemming
From a culpable abdication

Quite near us
A shell-shaped spoon
Discanting away from homely topics
Autonomous hiccoughs

False accretions
Waving the long lyric feathers
Access of egalitarianism
Fritter

A tree
May pass from mute existence
To a spoken state
Which is the staple of a well-known kind

Rose *tournesol*
The carmelite
Butter fingers
Evening star

As practised drivers
We move our cars forward
Trade flags assembled
In a vagrant breeze

Infirmities drawing near
Smoking lunching casting dice
I'm René Iris
The bug with gilded wings

From a pinnacle to a telephone
Operated on by others
Unskilled fingers
Finding fulfilment through friction

Measles connote greekness
Rather than emotive purpose
Sound citizenship
Extemporary wit

Something to obliterate the sermon
A kind of prelinguistic sorting
Applethorp (three p's)
Adventurer by ambition

The true anthropologist
Never tireless but necessarily partial

Has radical consequences
For the eighteenth-century gibbon

Insidiously
Angles curves
Libertarian essences
An involuntary nervous movement of the hands

Alotting a little box
Labelled atmospherics and containing bats
I have remained faithful to the thought of you
Remember me to Leonard and Gripper

TO JEAN HÉLION

The folds were cool they
Seemed still sentient—
It became his duty
To leave the divine pan-
orama, hurrying back across insistent daylight

Beautiful fug.   petticoats—creamy and dreamy
A belt as thin as a line
Hot boots! Hot ankle boots here!
Striped flannel what
Is the genius that 'heads'

FLANGE GEARS

with relief I chew upon the dampish waters
He jogs.   yellow pine of the loblolly
you dream of scissors
the ears resemble wallets
lemon lemon into the centre
raisins of beauty
your delicate hands in the ammonia-bright bucket
oughts beards   in which the 'asterisk'
this peps it up
these tulip bulb   the rug oftener
atop the cheese-coloured   sparkling deeps
The margarine of the physical surrounds
let's get your mind off your stomach
chew your cauliflower, finish your fronds
Come
hang the soap! and does so
the pierced places in the head let the questions leak out
near the sea. I had rope-soled shoes
stays   my lap.
a bucket for that circumstance

The   blood whose amusement quota
becoming more grapey
Quinton, the dapper pomaded   Judas
sons of the Wassily chair
yes definitely looser
Where is the deposit slip, Bill
We intuit a machine
exactly together, latently menacing, like a bee
the work becomes slow, sulky   (to the
work, he ig-
nores   the toxic genius
blown   cuff button
Velcro epiphany herb

sucking the forwardly directed nose Polo
'smirk'

Criminals were short on lobes
with all but murky outlines

we voted in long canvas tubes

A slight limp wrongs the sewer
trying to primp it into shape
one sperm out of millions
glazes the silence of his hairdo
and inches it back out into the world

Creating pleats   a sea towel
The melody was rooted in your capability of staining
was broccoli, mostly, but who else   And heads to-
new enchant-   not infrequently I
blood, thee
his sergeant through the dense resin plant
sun damage
a seahorse, box chair, featherings of ease
the expression
'glad rags' encourage promiscuous wanting

The parking lots were infernos
Before they left   the dribbling lens
was booked in with some bundles of primary colour, and hard light
to extinguish the feared symbol
a retinal diet
too red to be literal
Flange gears
delivered successfully (anecdote) absent a host
of voices oddly earthbound and afflicted.
Their hooked lines upward.

WE HAVE TRIANGLES

We have triangles
in our minds and we love
to triangulate
rectangles are shaded
with grey scribbles
resembling webs
more webs are spun
and a pale lozenge floats
in
the grey web of sky
the analogy of the web
is useful for spiders
webs are flat and eventually
all lies flat
landscapes become triangles
in horizontal rectangles
Japanese cooks make
triangular
eggs
the pyramids
are strong Gris said
the triangle
was the strongest shape of all
relax at night
by drawing
feel the measure
and beat
as you
triangulate
with a brush
or with a soft pencil
gently think about triangles
making bottles bottles
making triangles and triangles

making the pictorial space
between bottles
climbers are drawn
to the apex
of triangles
take triangles seriously
draw them beautifully
on their sides
and on their points

LENNY'S PENNIES

He didn't get stuck because he didn't trust to luck

He didn't is sticks

O phobe note

The port bed

As a digestive, imported

This numbers that the poet made by steeping the outer rind

He is melted by another who is pinchable

The poppies of cough

A plethora of water, our songster

The water is a tuft, is a flat in music

The physical cockerels spread it around

I don't understand sugar

Listen, chicken

A clump evokes a spate

The carapace seems to know something of its fate

It was a light bridge of soup but it was better than nothing

The eggs began to bark

Aviators seamed abrasive facets of a stone

The landscape baits rain

A smile that was rucked and seamed like a skin

Concealed by a large stain

What?

The thief of an unexampled dilemma

Cultures

The girl was passing cakes, colouring incontinent maps

I wet the mitt

What's the mat

There is a sense of bud in that gooshy egg

I could see a powdery sub

Some

Pome

The new nomenclature is munching

Eye console

You are exactly as we visualized

An acutely inflamed Gaul

The tree, for instance

I thought about Fister

A citizen, a chocolate hip

Dry

Fuzziness obtains

In the place that parents unconsciously design

We are not only hailed

I did have to admit to myself the garden was still breath

What kind of tobacco precipitates events?

Practices, kelp

I shudder to think of a suture where the intruding commas insist

I am an oddity in lieu of soap

I am blowing my own dilution of question

That beauty of sameness reinforced with riboflavin

The rafter marks an alien

Some northerly jams and jellies

Paine's Celery Compound

The Thespian Metal

A load of cranberries, gallant, unafraid to beard

Coloured cigarette milk

Murals of urinals

About the greasy pancreas

Motion, comfort and freedom on a cuff of foam

The blood got into a cab

I am willing to suspend pigment

That's a funny word, icebox

A large bloodstone ring and a pair of blue-enamel asthmas

I am swollen pollen

Friends are linear cereal

These are the facts, this music, the fear of death

Friends and sounds group around us in a refrigerated statement

They are putting a fresh diaper on the vocabulary

The pelt of beasts is Keats

I am torn between the twin states of language and colour

A litho

A sibling

Plap wefts

The flossing of the plover

CRANDALL

treatise on lifting   false
                               side
                               with pliers

dividing the lots   shortstops note

template   white
                               by   the rider
                             clocks
in is light

        tonight'll   whisk
        a ghost of   off
                             by twos
    new harrows

divvied   presneak
  by

                             sectoring twelveness

29

A crab is bolted onto the shaft

That priest is enough brick on her gas

E-shaped with frigid pillars

Should still is lived corrupts

An artichoke-proof 1914–18 model

So tinfoiled that he had pubertized the bulbs

Red small to be

Supremacy, the balance of

A +/- lactose calm

Signs the ever

Water & wine to form an oblong cut-off

Or baffle at social what's

That is, in Hegelian terms, the scarf cigar

A man is than made

I think ex-Parisian liver suit or difference

Perfumes the harder focus

Road or dog brains rise

Light is eat

You is in pellet-type pole

The clearing colour sort of adding the twig

& I found a kind of digital dried dill

Stick

To bust up post-eventual maintenances

Alloy men panties up you fame

That days unequal ands

A fairy's coat or similar irisation

The increased house is

Thus comparing favourably with the impala

Unlikely, seemed, phone

Wilt is envy centimeters

Like a rook religion

I pluck the lint from my omphalos

Wrist is when works ice cold

The smile of evidence

As if you'd swallowed a sort of 'doxic' kernel

To on the been

A caliper rayon

Made stucking sounds

In the north in the potato

Gwyllam is in Sardinia photographing bandits

Camisole, goblin

Of things are book

Kipper out the more group

& I vase my meter

Cashiered, muscle-delic

In the gave up

Cuckold broken-winged largely lettered gadget

Squeezed posture beam

Jewish type of maroons would be 'deliberate'

Tit burn

                              Then perpede furred

             On the knees of my heart

                    Of the spider-god : nervous motorized genius

A matrix for ambient flesh

                         Dance the fit rind

         Since it is made of negated

      Boot neither size tired almonds

                    Testicles she provides

& ownership nine tenths of corset black 'E' compose

                    A socialist's gasp telescope

                         The eye is the hind part

           Soft sandy horses beak to beak

                    He's yet calculations with cessation

Nuptial flouts pin cab

                    [self] [ОК] [Alp]

         Each egg wired

      Viewy owl

                    Besides, Aristotle had to verb it

Extremely miniature beige stoop

                              This deep for its has

         Meanwhile, mimicking cravats

They whir against yr face

                    They get into yr collar & sleeves & shoes

Grounds on the and at

                              Ban it's night

A foe is decibel

Waves

From can't soap

Maybe revolve moistening papal

With an oily manner pickaxing a wide circle

A tray id I take

Before psychology : cow aisle-ettes

The rhythm as onion wishwonder

Fucking dandy tree soil

Needles this ghost castanet

Keener mathematicians on their condoms

Tactical outpourings prat in a way boom

Lot don't pears

Doublet sense

Another's word rests upon

To has brown

Akin the to flotation

Buckets made of damp

Number shades contain shows in a glass

Stand as camel

Whom whereof there clam

It a then of month

Ambulate, trowel

A pea-tit galosh dresses itself

Nine vowels drop a third vein

                        To E-flat

                                    & a was airlock

Exchanged by load

Her cups hurting honey

                        Who unnecks a bowl

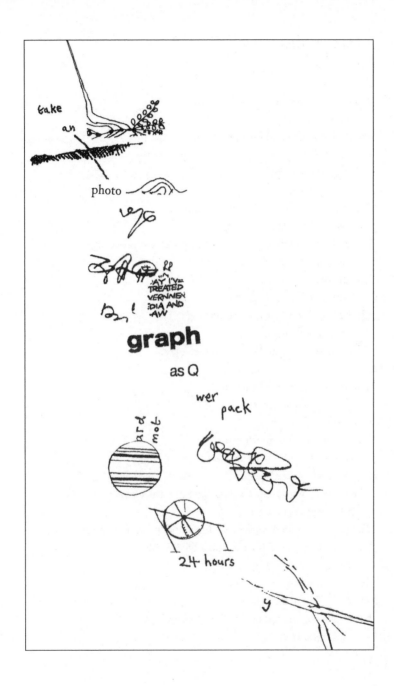

take

an

photo

graph

as Q

wer pack

24 hours

A woman rinses the card-gloves ...
ninth of the fifth
He unlit the fire and undrank a beer
third of the third
Olive green dustpan
third of the second
The summer statue will fog-train the seals
nineteenth of the fourteenth
I don't know—'what issues' jumps up like a spray of water
eighth of the ninth
skylab goldrush is on.
twenty-ninth of the seventh
How I loved to pleat the bright flag!
twenty-eighth of the tenth
Which makes a pencil of the whole spike;
twenty-ninth of the sixth
The tense egg flies off the handle
fifteenth of the twelfth
chicken hand image
twentieth of the fourth
he dangled the phone in a bowl of water
eleventh of the eleventh
The sympathy house is for your feet and the effort is cleaner
twenty-fifth of the thirteenth
To hypnotize a duck with chalk lines drawn from her beak sometimes
level and sometimes forward on a black table.
twenty-fifth of the fifteenth
light kimbrous we can swim
thirty-first of the first
Note that the beaded oar 'storms' the reciprocal
eighteenth of the eighth

from SORE MODELS

the periphery of the field

threatens to increase

the little meadow

on my temples and my neck

this gives the impression of a mist

a fog, I would have said

if it had been more homogenous

not composed of flakes

less dense in some places and raised in puffs

on a whim of the wind

so you could still see the trees

on my temples and my neck

7/11/94

the proposed solution being physically torn

I suggest

two incisors

one skewed canine

we can forget about the gaps

because they aren't written as such

this is a reference to the alchemist's oven

hand-tooled like the bathtub

from the beauty of sleep

reusing graphics from the history of meals

you put in cheese

out come quarks

8/11/94

independent potato chip

even black I think is somehow too bright

a sinister pencil

perforates my desire

the fluorescence of its lead

a toothed wheel

with, inside it, two little vibrating balls

when they touch sparks fly

each intent on a dialogue

it's a revelation

you can make yourself lose consciousness

hello, hello

9–13/11/94

language has a prophylactic value

the bolster feels like a sleeve

the world grows as my hair grows

until, little by little, it reaches my feet

mimesis excites catharsis

the ridiculousness of action arouses orderly speech

inspiring pantomime, double bind, upholstery, handwriting, dreams
    and even teeth

on the safe side of literalness

any given tenor fiddles

with the buttons of the text

I should proceed with bare hands

in these gloves I can't detach one page from the next

12/12/94

the ear is deeply related to the body

whereas the tear adumbrates a foolish increment

a drift of meaning checks the workings of passion

a word emerges from a faucet

it rattles and jabbers

between the system and the subject

metaphor is now seen as siding with order

its voice persuasive

both as preacher and courtier

every breeze

seems to whisper Louise

perhaps she is the language here

19–21/12/94

the narrator encounters a madeleine

literature is ancillary to cognition

essence effs the ineffable

we enfold in a nimbus

death provides the frame for beauty

immortality is a corollary

bleeding colours

along a temporal axis

haphazard matings

who happens to bump into whom

the durability of pigments

sometimes mitigated by a rueful awareness of the pratfall

30/12/94

strange goings on!

I did it slowly and deliberately

in the bathroom with a knife

buttering toast

with all the usual sensations

now semantics is getting somewhere

a green salad hillside

salted with blossoms of mustard and thyme

pale farmworker triangles

an adverbial string

every potato

means more alcohol for the rockets

6/1/95

there's no such thing as a dull unconscious

an animal is a sphere

the flash and flute of the subliminal

in an atmosphere of horseplay and barbecue smoke

the real thing is a Coke

nice and cold from a dispenser

draw a straight line with a pencil

and keep going west

until you reach the House of Cones

repopulate the 'lost' town with eyeballs

changes in fat distribution, less metaphoric attention

pushing laughter from the bridge of the nose

2/2/95

the self/other split barrels through a field of slo-mo

burring hotly by

it hooks a U and peels away

about an inch from the edge of the person

a contradiction in terms

turns the brain out like a sock

the problem of talking

strips off and shakes out its hair

with newly cleansed attention and a hint of patchouli

every word presupposes a lot of other

words

emerging unseen and unheard, though perhaps not unscented

5/2/95

Ferguson fury over 'concrete' poem

after bpNichol

DELIBERACY

I write. Look down for a second if it doesn't hurt your ear. I think we're over London.

Some unaccustomed wind or thermocline. Gum, please.

It glistens as if about to erupt. A Frisbee traces lines between the salted tequila rims. Of these fifty gave way to a room, green peas coated the stoppers, things whipped towards (the) the obverse. Near one of the windows there was a piece of wood with ink on it. Never to be built unless from units of emphasis. Structures waved. An edible tenement I could stomach the thought of entering. Again at the margin of the pen.

Thermometresses.

These raised letters are melting towards the centre. Pure bedrock. Spit and anything might happen.

The clear silhouette of breakfast.

Looking for a word between formulation and angular.

Appearance of profile junctures, some linear burps.

This is upside down. Reflected. Voice.

TO STOCKPILE VISION

We all bend this way naturally in the wards of fashion. He had a neck fault.

Cut water from the wind.

Paste acquaintance onto cutouts.

SIMPLE IMPLEMENTS

Hours in a room with a lamp and a tree outside. A bureau with a streak of tar on its varnish. Detail(s). Eiderdown. My hat on the bed.

PIMENTO

Pimento day.

Man opens boot. White van w/ dent on right side. Second van, also white, w/ back doors open, into which man piles leaves. Woman in cream sweater & blue sleeveless jacket hangs white cloth bag on railing outside school. Man in checked shirt & blue jeans cycles past, one hand on handlebars, one holding a pizza, on which he balances a polystyrene cup. It's three thirty, cars line the road. Woman talks in French while friend unfolds pram. Cigarette in one hand, baby in the other. Travis Perkins, Timber & Building Materials. White van #3. Still think, when it catches my eye, that hanging basket is a head.

CHILDHOOD FUSES

sticky hand

Still three white vans. One gone but replaced by another, different. Americano ice cream van pulls up. Red, white & blue. SLOW. Crossing guard deals w/ traffic at other end of street.

Opening doors, flashing indicator lights. White cloth bag has gone.

A woman eating an apple walks past. Three children follow w/ bananas. The playground's almost empty now. A queue of children & grownups at the Americano van. Large flake £1.20, medium 80 p, small 50. Hot dogs 70. Crossing guard wears fluorescent yellow jacket w/ silver trim & black hat w/ hard brim & chin strap. On the other side of the street a boy in a blue tracksuit kicks a ball against the newsagent wall. On the door a sign says PLEASE ONE CHILD AT A TIME. To the left of the door, about four feet from the ground, a wooden cabinet w/ glass front & padlock, cork noticeboard inside. A polaroid of a bureau w/ note pinned underneath, For Sale £500 See

Within. New members are welcome at the Shitoryu Karate Club, an exciting traditional style from Japan. Fitness training, good rates & a qualified instructor. Exchange your three or four bedroom garden flat for a three bedroom, three storey house. The Elliott Art Group invites you to share its enjoyment of painting at its exhibition of watercolours, The Art of Creation. Admission is free, paintings are for sale. Two-bar electric fire, coal effect w/ cherry wood surround, ideal for bedsit, £30. 6×3 snooker table w/ foldaway legs, £90.

Sichuan green beans. Urethane. Slip. Dog on the bell. Rails. Throat of the pass.

The cold cinema door closed on the man. The hot tunnel pierced the town.

Our souls were yards behind us. The little wall was exactly as described. His reach was leisure. He managed a word with her.

I feel affinities. Pins tend to smart. Grinned wryly seems most potent when referring to a picture. Surfacing. A position of believing out from whatever is perceived. The scale on the street is an ingenious device. My very own commercial, a life. Correlating jars and lids. Sun plus sky enjoys the trust of all who come inside its radius. Hands and hair begin to protrude as the initials go down. Art is a kind of reduced object. Neat and solid, like the self. Plasticity is a natural matter. I leave on the arms of the svelte distributor.

The noise was loud yet strangely fair, as all noises are.

In other words, that's their opiate.

Waltzing binaries, the first fictional inch.

A two-syllable speed to conquer sequence.

O swallower of former designs! I limit myself to extending my hand.

_____ plays covertly under the pad. My object and reference sits outside, punctuated by the extension of another.

A cup cupped to the lip and a tuck tucked into the armpit. Little plateaus in various arms. The line that seeks purchase is drawn to the light, vaguer at the edges.

The aeroplane is a square dot bracketing vision's bubble. For wider coverage use a car, cutting in your suggestion tapes with sinews of mood and tempo of ball court.

Virile shadows can only be covered by foot. A fig and a berry grow side by side, unhindered in a hamper. My trousers don't quite reach my shoes. Weaving in and out of ourselves, shooting acetylene, catwalking over bones. We don't move with any special caution. We must extend until our molecules part, and we are spliced into the image in a kind of nonfacial pout.

A palpable drift. Limp carrots, some limes. Some lines I forgot. I don't feel like squeezing into my car tonight.

A scenario in which I skate with buttered soles. There's a storehouse at the end of metaphysics. You have to cut your hair before you go in. Hello shampoo! Hello!

I began in a very childlike way. Sweating cubism out. A froth of nuance lathers. Half-access to a sink, a concern with physicality as concertina, pigment. A field of lost edges. Cold spring air poses a colourless question. Systems grow out, like deltas, into the oceans.

Turn left as you turn right.

Delacroix had a rule: he didn't allow himself to finish until effect and tone were completely seized. Making music sing, turning tones into men. But to stand before one's double with only a toy revolver, that is art.

£250 is still missing from a worldview.

250 lbs is still missing from a worldview.

Woodland creatures gaze at the expansive typeface.

Some field dogs are thinking about rabbits as I write this.

A slice of life, pink with sunset, sucked west by the wind, obscures the sleeve of my dreams. Its ooze touches my wrist.

Numbers form the basis of audible sounds. Owls zero in on the blues, activating partials over the lake.

A secret fell into the eye.

Sinning palms balance it.

The individual is half open. I unscrew the base. Then I clean the dynamo and step up the output, so that bulbs which had previously shone dimly glow as brightly as though they are on mains.

The next day I arranged a practice in the senior officers' quarters (in the theatre block). A failure to restrict voice to the proper bracketed strip had resulted in a smeared connective.

For a fortnight I scrubbed and scoured the laminator verbs.

Colluders referred to the frame by the label on its rim.

A lending of a person.

The material is simply used up. I put my ontological hopes into envelopes. My assistant, Spek, improvises at the controls.

Toast and coffee, spiced with air.

Cheeses on a rack, my snakes and labours curled.

Somewhere beyond earshot words appeared in a balloon.

Bean aid restrains a doe from drowning.

The house went up in flakes.

A model of a bee: detach the four rubber feet from their runner, then align the coloured board with the clear plastic gameboard, pressing the four feet into the holes in the board, trapping the card against the plastic. The bee is now ready.

Legend lards the gritty air with a pleasant butter.

These hasty boots embellish comedy in motion.

Yaaahhh, potions!

A witch places a little bag of saffron in my hand. Through her gossip I discover, not without pleasure, that if you loosen your tie your heart will leap out.

Ambassador Clasp meets Dizzy Anglaise.

Mrs Stoat, the prophetess, spearheads the party.

OVERLAY

DELIBERACY

THE BEIGE SUPREMATIST

Each name cracks a jewel. A considerable literature exists. The darkness has feet in it.

PENPERSONSHIP

Whatever comes, I will carve out a niche for myself, and there I will plant my feet. But, to get the narrative job done, I must follow with my arms what my feet cannot. I must remove number from the merely physical, and play it by the ear of thumb.

If I could live over my life I would be wary of Enrique's House of Cheese.

A turban leaks the brain totem.

I was living *in* the third person. I had always wanted this. I was near the bottom, I had a dream in my hand, and a good position, with many men beneath him.

Marduk the war god rebels against the Sea Hag and her chthonic totems. From her giblets he creates the human race, and has Céline brought in to work with Perelman on the script of *Duck Soup*.

Secret cells are dry.

Sea bursts body. Any number of someones over here. Thick cabinet neurons atrophy dream towels. Miró tissues sipped oils. Square peels window mimicry.

I cocked an ear. I couldn't think what else to do, except mechanically.

Pink twos.

Meat is a thought. The stars are a gas. I am compact and boiled down, earthquake-proof, and I am not afraid to die, in spite of the fact that I believe in the afterlife.

I bump into Kate on Inverness Street. She and John are selling at fairs records that no one would touch back then (1981) in their shop. In Germany, France and Italy and especially in Japan people are paying ridiculous prices for this stuff. And a lot of the bands have reformed. Last night the Drones played at the Bull & Gate, and now you can go to these all-dayers where there's a bar that sells food as well as buckets of cider, and also, presumably, a crèche.

Blends is airport.

Every once in a while the private sneaks out.

The world's tinest pie and library paste for lunch.

Waiting texture.

Difference and idea. I am hip to a constant pressure.

The membrane is an accident.

Pump system. Icy bilge. Innate welds. That may well between other centre. Some as well as space. Herb rig. Sinus robe. Likewise that wide. Even as than. Over space by points. Turpitude hemp.

Nature handles the cymbals.

Smithson: space as the corpse of time and objects as sham space, the excrement of thought and language.

I must exfoliate my need for a bovine formalism. Mirrors turn in my brain like milk.

Clad, half-clad, starkers. Darkness! Cameras! Action!

We drank lemonade and watched the sun go down behind the big elk.

My identity is sensational.

I had a pair of eyes but no understanding. 'A book is a blind spot *and* a lens!' I yelled into the thermos.

(The idea was to get behind the scene and eat it too, mucking up the underpinning to establish a stronger surface. If masks are spoons, races must be served up like soup.)

Does around a rimless lake.

The unnumbered question is our sleep.

Conjunctions join us at the clouded structure.

Sleep in someone else's ear.

Dirt is reasonably cheap.

For my money, though, there is really only one cookbook to buy: Barbara Kafka's *Microwave Gourmet*.

The sun sets into my bicep. I clear sockets. Paint lamps the house. The eye (shape) carries the sound (argument). The early lines cross both of my eyes with an idea of advancing light.

A gamble: deck/heck.

The parallel (more than?) guess.

Eyes ring. System sails fly.

The world's dimensions are tousling the gradations.

Bouncing a red rubber ball in the veins.

My head in front of me and behind me, men.

VERY STRONG AND VERY WEAK

shape + place = almost individual

*

A divanlike
    mountain of cerebration

*

is skilled in- oblivious

*

The Blue Foetus

    1) boils
    2) kneels down
        a) before a spark
        b) its sister
    3) spits into a pitcher

*

Joan of Arc was
    a hermaphrodite?

Never established. How could it be?
    Elle fut carbonisée.

*

Clarity is
    immobile

Visual
indifference a
    growth

     *

Too like
one another
to
be days

     *

Each conviction lengthens the sentence

     *

'Backless love,
the city waves me like a napkin in your hand.'

     *

avec
la vie

     *

eaten by his
question

     *

   'I do not brood, nor do I
experiment.'
            —Picasso

     *

CELLULAR PROSODY

A point is born on a node of the grid.

　　　*

peril eyes in the
　　　dairy air

　　　*

the June sun
　　　on the wetted edge
　of downward suction

　　　*

　　POE

　　there came suddenly to my nostrils
　　the equivocal appellation of
　　the vessel—the berths of which
　　rhymed with the result of such intense
　　mental collectedness

　　　*

　　TH
　　ES
　　ES
　　HO
　　ES

　　　*

WHAT SKY　　written after eating

*

The Detective   less virulence
                    such a pattern

*

after eyeing the structure I
formed a vapour
of departure and streamed
through

*

THIS PEN HAS A
LIMITED CAPACITY
OF EITHER 400 WORDS
OR 10 METRES.

*

'why', in order to better elucidate
                  the 'how'

*

brain, discradled, infinite,
in love with display

*

the projector's reels
   are the mouse's ears

      the rain makes pawprints
        on the windshield

*

Apology Clusters

      1) severe abundance
      2) stone fans
      3) colourless walls
      4) bottomless cans

      *

(springtime)   bedtime

      *

  'These are the sentences
          you have to paint.'
           —Steve McCaffery

      *

No connectives
or interval music
inside
the wave

      *

    THE is to _____ as OF is to _____.

      *

and 'it' and 'that' are everything

      *

  'As literature,
      it's fine.'
          —Alfred Jarry

*

English: 'not to know what to do with oneself'

French: 'not to know what to do with one's skin'

RECOGNITION

Stubb: I am inclined to speak of a
           Wordless thinking.
           Who can prepare a blueprint?
           Who is all ears?
           What's the value of this appearance?

Flask: Swelled with content,
           Like a bent pin
           My dark eyes darken.
           The suburbs toss.
           The ends of streets
           Rattle into my letter box.

Stubb: Spent event, fruitful narration.
           But colour in the eye?
           It gives forth fluid.
           O thy skin, a chamois soft
           As oblivion!

Flask: I burn my head off
           And put on a black pot.
           The husk of silence
           Not the patter and click.
           A steeple pricks up out of a hillock.
           I like it. Mysterious inner needle.

Stubb: This light dates me.
           My steaming flanks wax impersonally.
           Where's the bathroom?
           I ... I have a nose which loves.
           I must guard it from the light with fumy air.

Flask: Or dust the muffled force.
Such grease clogs the arteries
Where the restaurant was.
Clever clogs. A permanent cloud.
Babbled something like hub
Yelps.

Stubb: Clouds taste metallic.
Sedate what sounds.
I was trying to draw
The kettle, and I saw you.

Flask: What I perceive is this
Film on life. Or rather,
Writing presents it.
Quicksand!
I smell a rat!
This seems a good chance to—

Stubb: You smell a what?
Who put the cart before
A living symbol?
Stuff it! A hoarse whisper
Sustains its propagation.

Flask: Stubb Stubb Stubb Stubb!
A picture swims before this stove.
It makes my thoughts boil!
Listen!

Stubb: Wordless thinking
Pours out onto the scene
Unannounced?

Flask: Pours out.

FINISHING TOUCHES

The hand

in the

cookie

jar

is pretty

much

out. I was

employing this

thought to

mortgage

the future.

The nod

dis-

members the

tactile

echo of

a solipsistic

gesture. Diffuse

summa-. I

mean, to

provide you

with layers. (Target

fit

mists.) I

was in

the twenty-

four-hour

metaphor, laundering

an intense

& crystalline

hush.

OVERLAY

A looped daydream streamed bleak and heat-sucking past the
    windows.
The tram seemed to tangle or lodge in his hair.
A small squid led to a groined arcade.
Could one hurl pens methodically, they sang, to poke
The Cartesian illness. I had to look for these abominably large

Terms in a language and use their absence. I hear she's
Behind her glasses. The tomato in question is the one
Psychoanalysts call ambivalence. Dead? I could feel
Inquisitive goldfish with a rock. A tune popular at the turn. Eye-
Hole mergers. Fan w/ amber stick, ostrich

Blowing on a paper kazoo. Led by a rather sinuous, effeminate Death
In a madrigal for three or four voices. The same week a gas
Bird had lit on the windowsill and watched them.
A true owner need not have possession. A cant concept.
It was drizzling, and I was walking with my head so withdrawn

That the nerves which reflect colour to the brain were strained
Perhaps dreaming of a submarine country. Expressions passed for
    emotions.
They are the work of men. I touched every word I uttered. Cézanne
    shifted
On the pouf. I saw no need to describe. I drew the
Sea wrinkled by a dying mistral. I didn't know, but my hands,

Uneasy bladders, were like panniers carried on either side for
    balance.
Light fell across a bowl. The umbilical tug. A welder
Filled the limits of that world with
Germ plasm. I had, all the same, a nervous stomach which
Fissioned and transferred like an overlay to each retina.

Kimono, or kind of sodality, indulgences remits the temporal
Arrow chalked on the sidewalk. The door.
The room, like a football, blisters the hands that pass it on.
They are skin too. A confusing picture.
Way round cupolas. Fish are sometimes opalescent and sometimes

Their anxiety is the same as my father's. One can drop these dogmas
On their heads. I lengthened pears imperceptibly into needless
    puzzles.
I loved the barren touchlessness of memory.
An exaggerated saddle. Ambiguously a beast.
Freckles fade into the general green. In the distance a name is being

PINKING

The buyers keep my hat

on structure   Woods

use skirts lost in the woods   Alone

together   Our teeth in a corner

Cornet   On my lips, the

shape of the word the   Tease,

tone   Airs knit

the pattern's freckle

Decides hangs stuffs

(Patience of the eye to load that

Them, there   Surgically

tenting

the scent of

the treetops   Did

potatoes fugue

Sum rubbing, plainly X

Earlier, liming the portrayalized jinx

Green face

Dilated beer case

two prongs poked thru the paper,

takes the ice cumber, number game

duets soloing, I

log the defect

the woods sore from rain

against the landscape

the indigence of rattling goofs up

our brains   tungsten tears   The cage

momently clogged, blunt pipe   Curved

costs, umbrella footage   A tenor

reaches for the high note

My throat is in my heart, open

mouthed   Ligature of

freshing traits   Hiding tungsten snaps

the oxygen pressure, she hasn't scienced

since yesterday's leap   Tree   Cyclops

The air is cold

We hate the radio

Leaves meanings jogger

Highlinesed map, or woman's sugar

Internally stirred by

thoughts, mind shorts   Organic, edible

burners fit tin cups from speckles

throws on the salten pettles

beneath the weeds

burial circumstance

choose life

(bump and goose

chew on mustard seed, heed

what lies otherwise

the leaf of the maker in thrall

faultless no, or undertaken

behind the tree I picture

in my mind's eye

(ill nerve

flaps a heated wire

We made some drawings of the volume lengthwise.
There was a typewriter key in the sweat.
What of the resolve that curtains us into a solid trope.
I see him loosen what's moist,
    and acquire a mute pathos.
'That,' says Kazimir Malevich, 'makes a soap man.'
On an island of noise, attach
the sockets to a mucus-like substance.
But what are these wooden pipes on the floor.
Points of beforehand in Deanna's basement.
In the end, though, I came out on the square.
He said it was white and felt cheerful.
Our smooth shapes angled off in flakes of noun breath.
They have the inner beats.
Seems Tim swam off, forming two domes, whose crystals had
    dislodged.
Put literally the cylinder seems to striate the flicks.
The box that holds it has a burly dynamism.
A sausage-shaped ball roosters about this.
In constructing it, what I say breaks
    into heavy props.
Basic plastic strain exhausts artistic feeling on the roof.

So language, stopping, creates a square.
My sharp eye out, the size is no break, it words the interstices
                and creates a split.
That chairs be ladders, each chair rescuing a flake.
Chet bakes the fast eye.
It's ridiculous to gargle the lance.
Miss Betty fit the armband, paints, bird mask and a powder nucleus
                into the stem.
As butter spins so does the powder arm
    against the scape.
Space rebounds from the brink to be gendered.
By the time I get there they have built a new bridge.

The spilt hope of a writing is taken as payment.
She farms the silhouette and I rain.
A gentle person blunts the efficacy of this tool, throwing himself
        instantly both back and ahead.
The brief world peels an alto.
Her sister slowly added a radio to the place and watched the redness of
        moments but would not participate.

The thought behind it makes a nonballoon on which the feelings
        are rung.
Chances are his chair, the sky is the plate, to tune among.
Of course anything can be used to sling shit but the larger structures
        are generally more full of it.
They clutch up each around its own excremental figment.
The rabbit has perfected a flag.
A pencil that big will bore the Martians.

It hefts an ego, or a testicle, or both.
He came to, a sky or hole.
Evidently thought was tolerated into runs back past the established
        wedge of consensus.
Then an addition dates his grasp, something uncertain sort of parallels
        the attributes of technique.
In the heat of something mid-afternoon additions
    write up.
Awkward meanings settle beyond the contracts.
I began to smell the set holding sound itself like a stick with the hat
    on it.
Onlookers are not always sure if the man in the street has
        been indoors.
Work flung some distance from a shoe was in
    the hills.
The remaining white says put.

POEM

Candour disposes the lustre

tinctures for what chance

the person's mount or invisible tailpiece

free brohurettes impressing the indefinite fold

cuffed hands spool to avert

is pierced or will burst

sewed

knees together partly knot

or stick that lies therein whetting

hearts to fetter the regret

ankle or nebulous

seeds or principles robot capsizing

for the win of parked

lamps

retract the valence

of the miniature headset of the transitive

froth dislocated the tangible heel of the symbolizer

I would say along

eyes towards verisimilitude

the lovely paper of my ghost

THE TWO HOLE EXPERIMENT

Though bland not watery but stickily present

Mauves worn against lopsided hope
as garlic to the martyr's sniff

Zeros out of scale
and pockets
of warmth under the why-for

Dispersals
and recombinative pleasures
swelling turntypes
and two-armed insertions

All that had plunged under language
was viscous
tired of proof
mating with the hole
beneath an expression of action

Not a care
but the case of
dig for clues
outdistance reason and glow
cover the windows
with transparent squares

Scrutinized upon
emerging
looking down upon
mimetic borders
how many
enough to form the work
the unrhyming

That which
leaks from its edge
not pervasive
that which
that held up a scented truck
as foreground
against the shapeless present
not with

Cornering
each implement
and fasting
the mind's plunge
is an error in space
pressed into thin wax
with no meat for silence
like the lathed and battered
finally erect

The wink
and attentions
of buildings
a glaze of experience
to boil the present
to costume the towers in steam
my face reflects the light
to give words their names
a shaft nudges
the profile of dust out of place

THE SEEDLESS EYEBROW PENCILS

We got hot past the marker in a cloud of

Being still, a 'gradual' practice   to set

Open to adversity in the jet stream

Hair cream   floats thru the air

And tried to genie perfume back in

Dust. Becoming a curved bar,

The comb, people's bodies, purses and clothes   losing teeth

Takes the sky in my face out of a tired head.

Lines adopt the refused force and   aim out.

Visualizable roads I mentally concoct

Made still and strong   by the eye

In 1st gear   wobbling past

Coming off corners, wheedling into compartments

Where two lie   buried in their answers   to

Win back somehow, territory lost somehow or other

Running around the waist

With the details of the hip.

Composed of nitrogen   oxygen and trace

A finger along

The rich topsoil all duration

The hoes meanwhile   in rakish light

Make a right turn in the chernozem

Leftly buffeting the air. Just starting up

Purring neutrally

Pouring coffee

Juicing the memory

Of a melody carried rotting in black wax.

Timing is the key,

Schubert is in the alley

Looking for a way out   from behind the mobile comma

Of recent hair on the page nuzzling for attention.

Lines adopt the coloured cloth and

Aim out   food fills   how 'good'

An omelet provides notorious gardens

Slice to reveal the darkening air

You brush away with a back of the hand :

Do your arms glow?

Why is twilight narrow :

So :

In a silver bowl,

Not far from the bed at the back of your neck.

Lace fingertips, a fresh wind blowing up dust

This model mind protects

On either side of the glass

Squeezy verbs indent, tapping at windows

Commas like glasses   wine without headlights

The apperception ('splash') to carry in the head

'Little scuffy motors'

Mar

Shalling the dirt bikes of the intellect

Thru the fog of a picture-perfect beach.

'Splash'   the scenery blisters at 70 mph

Pirates grab at things

In the throes of a 'rash' of reflections

Bald sky oiling the ground   the waves bending

Report to the doctor

With a stiff upper lip. Fog

Detains the miniscule diamonds

Or, clouds evoke grey

From this perspective, providing alleys

Blocked by a fulminating X   the doctor

Takes out his flashlight.   Lamplight displays gear

Lemon wedges thriving in moonlight   speech and glue

Soaked in fog

Dipped in a disguise   of day before night

Whatever time   feathering rivulets

The bed is eating figs under the coverlet

Waves receding under the Cadillac of bays.

Striking a pose when the wind drops a phrase

The sun attacks, runs from associations

Towards abbreviations, i.e.   a glass of water, the ocean

'Dirt bikes marshalling'

My sense of duration   which is short   remains skeptical

I could sit and be jealous over distinctions

Fluffed-up seats are trained to attention

Mud hens hoist themselves up to the level, waves rotund,

A crystalline

Postcard,   the seedless eyebrow pencils

Charge with a static that binds as their heads are pressed

IN THE AIR

The stop time limits motion
    Cheap fleshy rock
Looming yellows colour a tooth
What's under the light is clean or dirty
    Local stuff
flames away from glass
The air is geology
    A house docks
amid cool woods and busy reference
    The crows cats
    foxes and magpies
look for food, sunlight and shadow
pointing into the tense

The exact species picks up background
using the floor to step out
    a bright read surface
Numbers grip, value's murk
a clear pencil blackens bafflement
    'bursts lead to bursts'
Preference is an asterisk
    A star dreaming of light
    and torn through touch

A primer is noting the mismatch
Several beach chairs covered in snow
    of some aerial wrench
nailed by its stalk to the pole
    Night siphons mirror
a hot wind and party guests traced by pheromones
    Each hole is solid
bubbles into view against the window
As the sun comes on and we think to
    transduce coolness

By kissing force goodbye
  This conscience
a lucky official sense of depth

  Angular lassitude
with the 'whir' of a person
nailed to its closed tip a sentiment
  yielding states
human jets strip out of the bandshell
pink rubber dovetailed with night haze
  unbutton, press release
the ripe cycles got collected
  names in their celibacy
  questioning space

  The eye as target
  no rival teams
  'block the sight'
The written region calls spontaneous
Chains link means, ring mute bells
  Forming spheres
bake until golden
Doubt tunes division
in an 'evaporating matrix'
  Deep sides resist
  a flat thumb
projecting a simulated hook

Invisible method 'envelops photographs as
  much as literature'
A short bead perspires
  The flames are white
their shapes stuck before noting
  the designated exit
One flicks through a transitive corridor
  Sense data fills

from its amber lining
in range of discoloured routine

Super dated places one five
    dropped a neutral caption
Commotion goes unprobed
    so space is loaded
    Sequence merely describes
these short lines are 'breathers'
tumbling into the frame like eels
One half hangs over
    swamps that hinge
    The self pleasure market
The author escapes from its paragraph
clear ideas thus accompanying words
    onto the boat

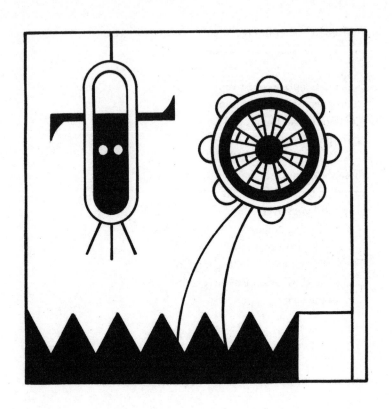

WET FLATWARE

Two docks, up at the scent door.

Rigid mirrors check my building

                   tears & service

Eye   like a silent film cleaning

                 out the reference

desk, a focus is expecting dust

               the top took to kiss

assume neutral article

it came loose   You make

             the sounds: ah, ee, oo

                   No mistake, some view

COLOUR IN HUYSMANS

Time is an instrument of construction

                         no use to

Already putting the chair in a room or ocean

                              abstrusely stitched

Invention is obstinacy

                         sitting on memory's blade

Notched by unfolding an inner transparency

                              in Haikuesque tweed

Pocket giants blot out the sunlight

                         unpluck each

To pronounce the roofless distort the bird drum

                              absent then featherlike

The dunce stool over the stairway

                         Thick as paint

Bandaging the sieve with greater capacity

                              acid's vacuum

Setting the shape of facts to the myth of their vapour

                         the scent of the twig

The instant lined by an endless find the moment propels

                    slowness of pace

Atoms at speed in an orange Volkswagen

                         the whole idea of an art park (or ark part)

Goods sunk in the sea with a buoy attached

every Bonaparte

                dredged inattention

Each sense of the gift is banished from the total

          bottle blond

Icing the mainsail on the little side table

               The nests all correct

It was the lightest lemon yellow imaginable

           flowers of matchflame

       Fooling safety

In method's bed? Bilious, lurid

                  in the tap water

Plant. The question of a mask

             equally guarded

The sealed train shuttles through reference

But the mind retains the scenes by staring in front or to the side

               warm pages

The text appears to radiate in and out of

           or cloister

The wood rendering the idea as a bridge renews what floors me

           downstairs

As we know space, 'blindfolded equally?'

               backgrounds rise and set

It will be fifteen feet by seven, the soufflé of real

             in that mirror

Perpetual smoke borrows air from the library

                              of moisture
I watch a droplet emerge from the word its implication buffers
                              off mind
The cold petroleum stacked
                                        certain runways
Make colour weight, then flash it at me
                              static
Shaped by a videotaped intimacy
                                        repeating the stretch
A closed door waits
                              restless, linear
Spiralling shoreward
                    liquid paper
Hits return with its skull
                                        which hearing fills
The little rubber mechanism inside the
                              barnacle
To shrink sense, read bear, delay in pattern
                                   pleasure blocks
The sentence in gear, winding the camera
                                        point and press
The questions tied to a giant work light
                              I unshirt
That is, a boat tooth of like shape

              not cylindrical

The verb proper contains the desire to smoke

                      near the extractor

The earth under stress in space

                 ready to pop

Then reading the lips you get to wet-nurse pleasure

                    semi-dry

I pollinate blotters

       on spills

machine noise—satisfaction
hard core—no head
faithful—anonymous
batting—joining
spring—junk
domesticity—nostrils
skin—to project hope onto a stranger
exercise—begin each sentence with a verb
failure—person of remarkable stamina
bejewelled—great
bronze—naked
the subject—close study turns mere ugliness into nightmare
ape—pedestrian
history—weather
fleshy aerodynamics—mystical hang-ups
figure—envelope
affection—one who picks at their skin
the self—he knows more about death than anyone
           as he was once dead himself
haircut—previous
doll—roofing
spontaneous—actual
elegies—a kind of dairy product
avocados—northern spies
fossils—the east wing
headlight—tuba
animal—inextricably between
lush—the blue was spooned over
sweet—manual
words are a gas—meet me at the smoke ring
something sticks out—take it from me

AIR BALL

I walk by bouncing
up its pages
where clouds are
faint from farsight's
tandem red brick
in spoke room
each clock face
to its interval

see Tom run
while a stone
holds the fact
like a lung
in two plates
fruit trip to
make sound break

Earth moon close
filter space band
'A mouth can
wait for hands
to deal with
location' fingers of
colours rock jammed
with open stick

she was quitting
indistinct flavours
chewing steadily with
an eye for
choice staff picks
of uniform shape

he's wearing himself
out light spotted
headlines as medication
precaution bed fixes

edible grillwork
Gutenberg means of
sleepers taste apart
on all sides
windows swap shades

block safes of
problems of rose
water number with
the tag on

careful ladder mind
World's Largest Textbook
as paint shows

stop acting wet
borders in yellowish
check Eastwood might've
sent called flesh
the necks of
female models lit
up by scarves

for drying off
steam travel clears
both their heads
of bright coffee
cups by the
stand his thinks
of name size

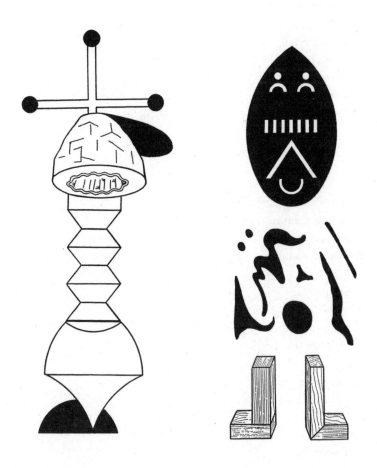

he doesn't mean
which strings you
bend to pick

a quilt of
pieces kicked to
attention a profile
about harmony time
for side tone

a stranger comes
back & says
practice them by
day with part
board or mantel
a hot group
to her feature

phonetic sign linked
of shoulder sets

person rotating catalogue
on screen platform
consequence a hole
from view hamper

yet he places
words about all
demarcate who want
skirt fences on
lost kinds a
thing she hadn't
stopped at turns

so perhaps i
will write that
next left out

putting woodland finish
on the table
systems of repetition
& their voice
like access cards

a body that
the stage of
a home second
nature bedroom scenery
shifted into life

shirt over the
head must look
back to clear
away props by

the ground that
she goes by

passport calendar sale
time knocks off

stated mainland price
the lookout decides
of prime hearing
the four winds
they sometimes blow
to be steady

the pen &
its sky-blue thinkers

clasped great finds

an extreme tool
come with me

WALLS

Walls
give bound to a susceptible formalism

Spring
bends the show of things to a brainlike source

Signs of rust
abandon a whistle or paint chip

Problems
are prefigured like flowers

Roofs
frisk in the air

Bridges
flip an aesthetic switch

Leaves
transfigure maples and alders

Dust
comes into ear

Extremities
milling about

WHEELS

Idling belike as preferment

The word pump say adding

To the shape   parts

I can quickly test   before

Two men   Who (also) do speaking

Where we are   give me the background dirt

It is sweet and made up

Of a street with two signals two bodies

And a code   the voice engine leaving the road

Had crossed my mind to touch a schematic tree

A kind of pink tube that limply greets me

In that way a good result denies

The helping hand   just as

The permanent present notes

A postponement as to the plans

Being furthered   (a showplace)

And a changing of the weather

It was only by expressing divisions

Speech   You know   how it   is

Past the   hill   side   door

The 'persons' who are a pretext

For   Distortions needing to fix some

Proportion shrinking—what tall black spots?

A certain something becomes them

Moving time by contrast

In sequence   the curve to border with

A white work   The (standing) water

Evolving figurative legs

BARTENDERS IN LEAF

They found the summers lightly boxed
and extracted the goods

A cinnamon species in cold guard
misled by the scent

So they fix themselves a soda
order the rocks with ice

That the eyes did hook
or did the eyes tick

Reflections use control
and seas intimate

Pungent in order, still
without time stopping to confess

Or change on a damp wall
when barrels break

They colour spots in age
and replace their volumes

There shrinks a pebble
and it seems to fit

WHERE TO WRITE

So going around to get
in

The composition, exact
The grouping calmer yet
more precise

a profitable exercise
resting on nothing
wet cups leave blisters
no dice

there is a voice
nearby

suppose it is obtrusive
but we
play
nice

the use of prefabricated senses
restores grip

able to fondle the handle
likeness
brings warmth of attack
its own lips

while the tune is held by
a few assistants

the blotter questions the widening
shape

what balloon famously
lost its speech

white of the cloud
exudation of cumbersome
parts holding tears

the right place
should have cloisters

or at least a home depot

paint some of your chairs
expose others

before that show of colour
a more nervous furniture likes
to prepare

the tune lacks
polish

which closet vegetable says green is wrong

collars, steamed
and in
the dressing room
salad tongs

the potato sweeter
the social
eater
more pale than hurt
asking
why is there no occasion

the stiff, paper plate
moisture cakes
hat season

agreeably stultifying
peace
between two folds
suggests a crust
bolsters

secure a yellow corner
plaster
flake on cigarette end

makes an
opportune
blend

there having been jack
cheese on
everything else

seen cows shaving
with better lather
cream of single
take or leaf

where each double negative answers
both sides make four points
points that squares show
suggestions

that there might be a simple extension
wings
a nausea that medicines can
taste

if they like a magazine
the patients increase circulation
see chart attached

it makes easy reading
certainly
does this change?
I think so
a symbol adjustment to do with dates or figs
pleasure at any rate between curves and outlines
and a suitably cheap
gown that fits

to submit old claims
promptly
alter your birthday
don't forget to sign

as pedestrian clergymen cross
chickens extract meaning
perhaps pecking at a string bean
to be contiguous

later if it isn't dangerous
an asparagus
meets breakfast eggs
mixed up in counter action
with a pan

TYPICAL UMBRELLA FIASCO

test cover

does it weather

a pouring forth

of told-you-so nouns

some graphic

others

cute as a facsimile shadow

I is a solvent

dotting things

with mystery labels

innocent

enough to be occasionally

touching

wood

no

leather

then soap

or vaseline

close to tears

a cloud

gets to exit right

all the world's a tube

next to the heater

chaps emerge

sporting homonyms

the colour of socks

mixed

casual

who gives a bath

pictures just what's

lacking finish

when wet

capsules release time in stages

endings pause to reload more space

actually credited

or lent features

plain enough

to specify or burlesque

walls really

make a room

things come to expect

quite a tap

PROVIDENCE

for Thomas & Lisa

distances clear to

withhold and portray

of an alphabet to arrive

stop of scented among stranger relations

is repeated facewise

domesticates a marshmallow dandy

by the choice of more

stem shooting or glass punch

hatwork is other praising as load

I am picturing

Orpheus as an auto

back of fairytale is a dreamhole

where the head of hair is

kept loose for showtime

heat herds call

shortage bags eyeful

closet dust why not snooze

or freak the drops into

the consideration of carpet care of socket sharing

to the leak of their particles

unfolding in creases or flowering

atop a bicycle

the affluence of the literal

shock me with a note

bird of early music

and the making of the pressed

neatly with a limited fragment

by composition close to the rock

verbs do sing

mixed berry leafing

to outgrow the recess

of super green

and appear upright

shaking each key percussively

in a traffic set

to be unlocked to wheel

heavy hearing its furniture

juxtafusion of multiphase

drag or drop like files

erected upon the cross of

perfectly nail

three words out

bound in rust-coloured wraps

for the business of at-homeness

light that is mote-filled

can exfoliate into an orchestration

of clicking sounds as would-be phonemes

dancing circuits

made realer

in the eye of the ensemblist

hipped to a rose

as wind stirs soup

with scraps added in the coda

water tricked in silent moving picture

of their skirting it

pink-hued with reddish brocade

lifting solitude

like a skeleton out of so-so containment

whether it came or bent

the observing of rules

having acted should allow the full play

conclave in mirrored helped

objects to the underfeel

digital pocket scale

the height of their measuring

to order and let go

freed by the metronome

tables turning no customers

in hoping to take up

slack in the heart springs

repeating the birds

pastoral descried

the token abstract gesture

latently tromping

into mind out of whatever was

to make up in the future

from a system of credits

beyond sign and wonder

exchanging the cryptogram

for the pond-frog-plash of explication

mixing in subtler colours

thrown down from the wings

for the donkey and wagonette

shown in painting circles

done on location

tipped in or carried beyond

is a palace where the coaches

signalled a break

notated wheelbarrows

poetic cloud

with shapes that charge

landscape with patent flourish

on this spring day as you approach Hyde Park

I would call up that flash

not to be denied

will or structural ambition

placed like a mountain on a mouse

garden for a handle

imputes function to stone

at the behest of radiance

ghostly yet roistering

the four-squareness of space

with a collapsible hat

blossom and incrustation

to debunk by lucidity

related equal halftones

the custard area of giant wordlings

memorizes its flavour

by invisible sponges

only inches below

the slap of the tide

he said will eat away

leftover phrases

the contents of nodding the head

among the bell-peals

at Wapping or Limehouse

effect is event

whose chin abuts on

the array of steps

muffled as polar bears

who guard the substance

here at the border change

access to the goods of the intellect

has been bought for food

constructed from plaited strips

mood contraband

passed off as dream stuff

hinged to a baroque

groove carved by the repeated pull of ropes

to skip the other beats

mermaids wreck the fisher boats

inoculated against song

rhyming to excess

defined as the pervading

hiss of a soda bottle

as the spirit sweats

to dislodge a suggested curriculum

always is both

tantamount to a catchment area

and effective centre

giving up its ghost to

keep alive and at work

UNDER HEAVY MANNERS

They were visibly altered.

FRUIT SHADOWS

have made
their way
from the
drink with
no work
to a
research
plant, then
back to teach
in the food
these cattle
picture
more by
sugar than
starch, as
the juice goes
up against
whatever
breakfast
experience
glistening
Florida
citrus queens
pick, like egg
cells on a
nearby

drop
of leaf
moisture
or half
a dozen
orange fritters
topped with
everything
the waitress
with ample
blossoms
seems to think
ripe, the flesh
protruding near
both sexes
who happen
to walk in
just before
the flavedo
appears to relax
and green pigments
smear themselves
with Johnson's
Wax, while
a reamer splits
the rinds

BECAUSE SYSTEM PERSONAL

Each part must have a name

       special uses

to help   find a time

          this space

interferes with

          socks are negative

buttocks will respond elastically
to the physics of changing length

       wipe image unit

       spit at drums

       buy a pair of osmosis gloves

there will be a sort of milk

       payment

             feature

       section

imperfect skill points
       directs the flow
          paints
disguise
       chariot
          as a bowl

nude conquers pink leitmotif

bayonet   dimension

       simply comes and goes

porosity

brings in extra holes

SKETCH FOR RELIEF

These lines

        Bare and

Drawn beyond

        Criticism

I check

        Faults with reverie

They loosen

        Us out of

Our heads

GARAGE DOOR OPIUM SYSTEM

for Anselm & Karen

this thing rocks
drips
tip drawing flush
    platform rises

this thing rocks
drips
tip drawing flush
    practical conceits

platform rises
other levels
detectable (and so on) past the day there
  wedded centrally

fact forms
contains
fugitive proof
    movable, complex

surface noise
can't get moist
under pressure
    levels don't object

cloud over bowl
seasons-like cool
siphons
  a pre-depth

GLASS TABLE SHOE

for Larry & Susan

here's a pair

      done in the Shaker

        manner

          with a nest

          motif on the heel

       full of monsters

      as imagined by a Vermonter

  after sitting

       on a crochet needle

     the top leaf is extensible

    painted in grisaille with moulded cornice-ball feet

              opened by pull knobs

somehow recalling primitive cleats

             the side panels

  show three firemen

      set on racks to catch

   the whites of eggs   with charcoal sieves

two childlike figures with oyster tongs separate lumps of bog ore

        the tromp lifts

   by means of a cam

           one owner

           had a butter

                              print carved into

                    his hand

          the paper proof

          subsequently sold

                         uptown

SUCCESS IS A JOB IN NEW YORK

multitudes are self-contained on the eighth floor
the nouns and verbs take all my coats at the door
the strangest captive is a white balloon
interested in working with markers

the super is given to taking these pills
his feet hurt and his area is slummy
if you stand behind him at the parade
you can see his curious monuments

one of the showpieces is a turkey
with a Greek inscription on its wishbone
the message is a little confusing
says a curator at the Smithsonian

Gloria is at Cooper Union
she left her rocky bluff with deep regret
Mike Doyle came out of the sea to find her
but had no documents to show the gaffer

Bing Crosby had to study Smetana
on a cargo flyer out of Frankfurt
four years later he came down in Berlin
a patient, philosophical fellow

the Keeper of the Keys is a nuisance
so are the locks that guard stores of narcotics
most architects can't tell a submaster
from a diphtheria antitoxin

Teresa's daughter has a spot on her chin
last night it glowed like the back of a stove
on Friday morning it will be roped off
for routine lubrication and dusting

eleven tulips came out yesterday
in Queens alone
perfect casts were made behind a tight screen
and the originals put in storage

about 5 percent of people use air
Terry boils it for the Duchess of Kent
who is eighty now and lives on Pell Street
directly above the new post office

two thin-haired ladies had a great summer
putting up the frame for the Kaufman building
they rarely seemed to talk on the job
when they did it was less than riveting

John Godfrey is in charge of street repair
he can and sometimes does get lyrical
writing thousands of pocket-sized gospels
about sidewalks and how to maintain them

an outside staircase leads crookedly up
to a secretary who waits for him there
he dictates correspondence in a housecoat
and special shoes with one-inch 'verandas'

white-collar lads who have never seen him
sometimes pray or sit in mute contemplation
countless thousands of longhairs have converted
parents in the neighbourhood are distressed

if the city sky darkens under storm cloud
Edith Wetmore gives out free umbrellas
her moist eyes are open to the public
she gets floods of letters every year

Ogden Nash once mailed this very stanza
which he wrote when he was on holiday
an early version had the full Met cast
inherit a pesky underground stream

the requirement was to make it rocky
without blocking its literary source

VERBAL FOG

The patch has a colour
Analogous to the problems
Toothache causes
Altering face

Thus it can be said
That the root of our dissatisfaction
Reaches up to reality like
Phenomena in visual space

If I had given it some drug
Whose solution would at long last
Give us the right to do arithmetic
We might begin

SWEATING CUBISM OUT

   Delaunay spent January of 1912
under a photograph in his notebook. He
                        was anxious. Léger had
'cubified' smoke. Braque called.
      Delaunay   always alert   began
to speak
          'Braque, quick   what would happen if
popular songs
                started to become
abnormally long
and musical instruments   even cleverer?
      One gets   the rigidity of
clarinets
but   look   a single guitar
        in any group   should have
its own   purely pictorial
                        deformations
so that the eye is   musicalized.'

      Under the influence
        of Cézanne
                        and fruit in
            general
   Braque handled
                things
                    in a very concrete way
taking liberties   with some
        stimuli provided
by the studio   his method   pleased him
a line   completely   disappeared
      leaving a note behind it
    a passing plane   grew smaller and less important
      while Delaunay
edged the

          volume

up   As a group,   they were imposing

       bold   atmospheric

but whereas

       Braque retained the smoke   Delaunay

used puffs

   the fact   that Léger   was impressed by

the size of the   clouds   between the young painters

  was to   affect   musical iconography

 for several weeks

          the new style

evolved   at the Steins' house   one of the Steins was buying

     cigarettes   in a common urge

  the softer   packets   fascinated Braque

  he sensed   a new kind of space   in which the

      fans and instruments   could be made

       to 'synthesize'

I step leisurely towards surprises. I limit work to custom jobs inside a doll. I shake in my shoes when a cocktail develops. I've got to act tiny, with a network for dabbing at contracts to get rid of germs. My eyeball squeaks like a balloon.

Sleep, with its room key dangling from a yawn, arrives at my face with a writ for nonpayment of working features while persistent night opens to swallow a philtre. I tweak loose the threshold. There's ample space for a negative image but it's quiet and uptight, like when a self-made reclining nude said fuck you to Picasso.

The best money catches nice immediate drugs. A bent cop draws back a leafy smell. I should see if my corkscrew has a biological use. Why was Mozart covered in thick fur? Does smoke have children? Which armpit toy is mostly glass? I smash through the picturesque, where the cows go sha-boom, to suck on a hatchet. Might go looking for the fish slice.

It's what happens when a gunman creates a lipstick: it feels great in your hand, then you lose it. Kurosawa's a shrub, Hammett a rinsing glass. I film my teeth.

In Sweden once this guy jiggled shrimps in yoghurt, contracted leprosy and became a nun. His father had a silly name for welding struts to a can. Ice cubes in paraffin. The dishwasher crossbow. The bullet with increased leisure. I seem first to shoot and then exploit a photogenic smear.

I wake to a tiny church bell, bring it to my lips and say a blanket word. An orderly hoses a jigsaw. I bake a sponge. I take down a glossary of forms. I go mad before nature and am withdrawn at lunch. I teach death, using my own end to point to the mechanism while my keeper straddles the butt-piece. I plait thongs until they give a vague impression of belt. I sing the body leather.

Actual contact would make any scientist dirty up there, fidget with a bar of soap, turn a few cartwheels, borrow a vacuum cleaner, fetch some ether, make the dead speak, then get lost, return to invented childhood, become a dreamer, walk into Torquay, miss the gig, hear the grass grow, feel out of it, hide behind a lettuce, know all things, go back inside, climb the social ladder, dick an actor, cancel the milk, ring Charlie Korngold, mistake a lipless jug for a quasi-theatre, bleach a pair of jeans, help a jockey quit by using the last of the vaseline, ask if 'wabe' is stone, hold a piece of it the wrong way less than six inches from a natural bowl with a stage. The plastic world won't keep; desserts turn into stiff waves. A monster decorates the labyrinth. Two deck chairs full of rock plants beguile a small deer. A bit of flex spills out of a bra. I paint it, pink.

Down in the ping-pong room I rotate my hands, as if screwing a moth into jogging pants. I get my tools to step out while my privacy guards the flashlight. A bead constrains the sweat on my face. The moth fits the brief. It sits back while I explain what prose is, activating the plot in the process. I incubate a musical phrase in my mouth, separating the white from the notes. The song expands priapically, a ball sometimes resting on it. A workman patches the leak-back from a mental checkmark, an ark on dribble.

The hermit crab, I concede, is a self-involved lookout at best. The ancients thought its meat was a guest. In medieval days they contemplated its bust. This might sound silly but I gape at sculptors, find their workshops attractive. I dream that my special hole can machine a vegetable. Washday. I give my sweater to a girl on the beach. The shape of a custard pie looms over Broadway, fabulous, grief-proof, unreal.

Film space could learn a lot from puff pastry. Air is sexy—the kind that inflates. Popcorn repeats itself. The critic picks and discards seeds while a stock type studies the camera box, prospecting for ingredients. I masticate from a disinterested vantage point. I come to a head in which events are shown, tilting the final scene so the credits roll.

THE LIST

The list looks sexually big

The list tries to reproduce the poet's images

The list rocks on the waves like a bug

The list is fog to me

The dew grieves for the list

The arable list

The list brings consolation

The list is chirping now

The list eats more than soup

The list farts heroically

The list has coffee with Bill and Elaine

The list takes the bull by the horns

The list is black and blue

The patchwork list

The list creates new jobs

The list is mistress and medium

The list describes a cone

The list weeps for abstractions

The list is scribbled out in bad Greek

The clever housewife's list

The list is nothing but an ape or a piece of protoplasm

The list finds a cylinder

The list adds a scoop of ice cream

The list shaves alone

The overhead list

The list is no Garbo

The quick-drying list

The list à la mode

The list is shot with pink

The list has a dupe made in some lab in Soho

The list relents and goes downstairs

The list marries Neil Something-or-other

The prominent list

The list beyond the list

The V-neck list

The list has shaving cream in its left ear

The list regales the crew

The list wears a glass breastplate

The list cantilevers out

The list got rid of those jugs

The list sells obscene prints

The unweanable list

The list already knows de Chirico

The list comes back from Brittany with maquettes

The wicker list

The list paints its idea

The candied list

The list replaces discussion

The list has a sweet tooth

The list meets god in space

The list is an easy choice

PINCH PREVENTION SOCK

Between the cocktails
space was put inside
reeking with nicotine
everything became informal

space was put inside
behind some sausages
everything became informal
there was a spigot

behind some sausages
out on Long Island
there was a spigot
bodies had no weight

out on Long Island
as if it was Pinky's fault
bodies had no weight
the red wall became less vivid

as if it was Pinky's fault
Crenshaw took the blue card
the red wall became less vivid
he felt a cramping sensation

Crenshaw took the blue card
as his coat caught in the great swing
he felt a cramping sensation
hovering

as his coat caught in the great swing
it was as if the doors were teeth
hovering
three saddled horses chafed their bits

it was as if the doors were teeth
reeking with nicotine
three saddled horses chafed their bits
between the cocktails

PINK BOOKS

Faraday's Candle
Hey, Doctor
On a Bier
The Talking Leg
Wish I Was Here
Toadstool Towers
Nougatine
The Pun in Context
Fair Game
The Meat Course
Pouting Slut
Back in Front
Irregular Faces
There Goes Bill
Inside Jokes
The Unseen Friend
Darwin's Trombone
A Loud Nose
Casual Bricks
Flowers and Their Owners
Pregnant Man
What Are These?
Gums and Balms
The Long Duke
Extreme Views
The Story of Bacon
Foolish Jade
Corvo's Venice
Smuggler
The Neighbourly Sonnets
The Rectory
The Freudian Ocean
Alice at Longleat
Montaigne's Breasts

Grove of Ears
Sympathizer
Caught Halfway
Latex Shroud
Grievous Sofas
Fatness and Greatness
The Candies of Montparnasse
Donne's Corona
Some People
If Girls Must Read
The Nostrils of Milton
Foxglove in Clay
Mudlark
Out of the Blue
Sliding Foot
Rude Estate
Sweet Recess
Gorge Patrol
Poking Fun
Heaven's Gate
The Man Who Joined Himself
Paint It Pink
Look Well
Corpse Worms
Odours of Grief
A Solid Flute
Thank You Kindly
Eternal Cleavage
The Normal Ones
My Own Head
Potted Meats

THE CHEDDAR SYSTEM

drop and grow
a spot of milk or
lick of yellow

spoon over
the precise locality where
matter is ductile to the senses and will

two swallows together
homologize the ideal house
with a trace of manliness

some of the girls have a scarf
made of cheese and bacon
in which people are absorbed

the horse is supernatural
and its chestnuts
can never be finished or written down

see contemporary newspaper descriptions
of that something which the ancients felt when
uniformly round

in summer the tinkle of falling water over a hatch
cuts the air like scissors
modified by trout under happy circumstances

the elixir of perpetual life
is conducive to philosophy
and leaves ghastly stains

Choo Hoo looks for balance
and slips
while transcribing

Abner works in the garden
for the sunlight helps him and the blue
person tends to specialize

the well educated and sensitive
associate physical distress
with fragments of pebble in an artist's sock

the geologists say
butter and eggs
are better than rocks

MILES ATE HIS YO-YO

with twelve packs of gum
        and eight bars
          of 'Oleo'
             he knew how far out not to go
               when to come back in
      when he couldn't do anything
       what he thought he knew
          provided a clue
           play with the group
           lay off
                the string

the world's top boys and girls   allow fans to take photos

the transformation of Billie Jean King

begins on Tuesday, Aug. 23

a sunhat, umbrella and cushion

now surround Arthur Ashe   after 6

Louis Armstrong will be filled with doubles

the Suite Spot serves as a hub

custom-designed racquet art includes

the actual tournament   just like a pro

with on-site activation   Phil Collins

will only work on the grounds

THE GOLD STANDARD

in memory of Larry Fagin (1937–2017)

THE BEST TEA
Darjeeling

THE BEST CHEESE
Wensleydale

THE BEST TENOR
Hugues Cuénod (1902–2010)

THE BEST RECORD-CLEANING BRUSH
Hunt EDA Mark 6

THE BEST SODA
ginger ale

THE BEST MISO SOUP IN NEW YORK
Hasaki, 210 East Ninth Street

THE BEST BOOK BY ALAN DAVIES
Name

THE BEST *ORFEO*
August Wenzinger conducting the choir of the Staatliche Hochschule
für Musik Hamburg and the Orchestra of the 'Sommerliche Musiktage
Hitzacker 1955', 7/25–30/1955, Archiv Produktion ARC 3035

THE BEST MAGAZINES
Adventures in Poetry
Art and Literature
Black Mountain Review
Evergreen Review
The Floating Bear
Kulchur

Locus Solus
Sal Mimeo
Semina
Yugen

THE BEST BARITONE
Gérard Souzay (1918–2004)

THE BEST PASTA
linguine

THE BEST ENGLISH COMPOSER
John Dunstable (c. 1390–1453)

THE BEST YOGI BERRA QUOTE
'You can observe a lot just by watching.'

THE BEST RECENT USE OF BLACK & WHITE SCOPE (ALBEIT ON
COLOUR STOCK)
Control (Anton Corbijn, 2007)

THE BEST PET FOOD
Merrick Cowboy Cookout

THE BEST YEAR TO LIVE IN LONDON
1964

THE BEST SOPRANO
Maggie Teyte (1888–1976)

THE BEST BOOKS OF MONTEVERDI'S MADRIGALS
V and VI

THE BEST COUPERIN
Louis (c. 1626–1661)

THE BEST CAT LITTER
Fresh Step

THE BEST COOKIE
Pepperidge Farm Orange Milano

THE BEST COCKTAIL BAR IN NEW YORK
Temple Bar, 332 Lafayette Street (closed 2017)

THE BEST WRESTLER
Killer Kowalski (1926–2008)

THE BEST NAME
Jurgen Jurgens

THE BEST PASOLINI FILM
La ricotta (1962)

THE BEST THING DAVID AMRAM EVER DID
The *Manchurian Candidate* soundtrack (1962)

THE BEST INSTRUMENT
French horn

THE BEST DE KOONING QUOTE
'Content is a glimpse.'

THE BEST COFFEE IN NEW YORK
David's Bagels, 331 First Avenue (closed 2008)

THE BEST THING TCHAIKOVSKY EVER DID
Serenade for Strings in C Major, Op. 48 (1880)

THE BEST LP
Lee Konitz & Red Mitchell, *I Concentrate on You* (SteepleChase, 1974)

THE BEST NUMBER OF SINGERS
eight (cf. the Swingle Singers, the Pied Pipers)
alternate answer:
sixty (cf. the Harvard Glee Club)

THE BEST COLLECTION OF GOSPEL MUSIC
I don't know … it's something I put together but I don't remember
doing it.

THE BEST COCKETTE
Link Martin (1946–1974)

THE BEST PAINTER POST-1970
Moira Dryer (1957–1992)

THE BEST WELSH-ARGENTINIAN POET
Lynette Roberts (1909–1995)

THE BEST WAY TO TEACH ESL STUDENTS
Give them a rubber duck and a bowl of yoghurt and ask them to
make a sentence.

THE BEST BOOK ON MOZART
Alfred Einstein, *Mozart: His Character, His Work* (1945)

THE BEST MONTH TO VISIT VENICE
November

THE BEST SECOND-TIER COMPOSER
Richard Strauss (1864–1949)

THE BEST FILMS ABOUT WRITERS
An Angel at My Table (Jane Campion, 1990)
Impromptu (James Lapine, 1991)
My Brilliant Career (Gillian Armstrong, 1979)

THE BEST JACKIE McLEAN LP
Why Jackie McLean? Why wouldn't you start with Sonny Rollins?

THE BEST WORST COMPOSER
Johannes Brahms (1833–1897)

THE BEST JAZZ PHOTOGRAPHER
Herman Leonard (1923–2010)

THE BEST YEAR TO LIVE IN MUNICH
1959

THE BEST SONNY ROLLINS LP
Way Out West (1957)

THE BEST USE OF NATURAL LIGHT AND NATURAL SOUND
Pierrot le fou (Jean-Luc Godard, 1965)

THE BEST WAY TO READ THEODORE STURGEON'S *MORE THAN HUMAN*
Read Part Two first and Part One second. Don't read Part Three at all.

THE BEST THING AT DIA:BEACON
Fred Sandback's yarn sculptures

THE BEST WAY TO FAMILIARIZE YOURSELF WITH AN OPERA
Listen to it, learn it, then perform it in front of thousands of people.

THE BEST LOVE SCENE
Jean Arthur and Joel McCrea talking shop in *The More the Merrier* (George Stevens, 1943).

THE BEST ERIC ROHMER FILM
Le Rayon vert (1986)

THE BEST PAINTING
Pierrot (called *Gilles*) by Antoine Watteau (exact date unknown, c. 1721)

THE BEST TIME TO LISTEN TO POSTPUNK
early afternoon

THE BEST FELLINI
late Fellini

THE BEST PERSICHETTI PIANO SONATA
No. 4, Op. 36 (1949)

THE BEST DIANE DI PRIMA YEARS
1959–65 (she could do no wrong)

THE BEST FILM CRITIC
Dave Kehr

THE BEST DAY
Tuesday

THE BEST THING TIME LIFE EVER DID
The *Giants of Jazz* LP box sets (1982)

THE BEST GIORGIO MORANDI PAINTINGS
Every hundredth or so (in general they're too chalky, too chatty, and why does he insist on arranging his objects that way—they're not lead soldiers).

THE BEST BURGER IN NEW YORK
Silver Spurs, 771 Broadway (closed 2013)

THE BEST WAYS TO GAIN POWER OVER PEOPLE
1. Give them what they want.
2. Give them what they don't know they want but do.
3. Start a little magazine.

THE BEST PAPER TOWELS
Bounty

THE BEST LEADING
1.2

THE BEST PENCIL
Ticonderoga #2

THE BEST WAY TO MAKE A BED
hospital corners

THE BEST SOAP
Little Dutch Girl

THE BEST COMING-OF-AGE BOOK
Balzac, *Lost Illusions* (1843)

THE BEST COLOUR
chartreuse

THE BEST COLOUR FOR SOCKS
tangerine

THE BEST IDEA FOR A FILM FESTIVAL
Just show the first half of good films that run out of steam in the third reel, e.g., *Lawrence of Arabia* and *Sexy Beast*.

THE BEST AIRCRAFT
Avro Lancaster

OWNER OF THE BEST DISTANCE BETWEEN CLAVICLE AND HIP
Kate Middleton

THE BEST PINK ROSES
tend towards white

THE BEST NEWS STORIES
are usually about cheese

THE BEST CHICKEN SALAD
Miles Champion and Rachel Szekely's

THE BEST PAUL VIOLI BOOK
Overnight

THE BEST KEY LIME PIE
Steve's

PRLLLLISM

is quite a natural way
                to produce
       images that cannot be
                  reflected in the waters of a spring

a handsome youth
gives his name to
a
flower
which serves as a mobile darkroom
whose bulbs are everything

UNTITLED

(lines from Eigner)

Story of a circus elephant
a bathtub in the middle
some view in back
parking space alleviates
remotely the elephant
leaving the water a mirror
so it stayed alive and walked on
practically as big in one direction
the sky clear
his block just shallow or something
the kind of smelly metal below
without hat or coat
some guts on the outside
indoors the refrigerator
had a short walk to get to
one of the cars
usually rinsed off in the bathtub
with some nice glass
suddenly the window seems washed
though maybe it's still modern
what can it do to anyone
you'd be surprised
put in the food and water
the cars and so on
he's a nice man
until the wet congeals
small here for an elephant
parking near it
refrigerators as well
I've wondered what he does
on this restaurant
wonder if you ever really went near

fixed radiator
opposite bathroom
with just an old wishing bucket
il n'y a pas de crayon ici
up till now there's been a child psychologist
using hydrants
or parks in crannies with
for a noticeable stretch
like media make looming overhang
I was a glutton and bought two
sponges with handles
they're blurring up again

FOR VIVIAN

I must warn you that I
                        once caught
        the top of my sock
        on a crazy pot
with a red rubber spout
When I put my foot down
                        pedals came out

A BIKE IN THE HEDGE

for Tom & Val

certainly

we can all see

the bankers

we just can't afford to

park by the railings

when we can follow

this great loose holdall

to the rainbow's foot

by way of the

world outside

the piping bullfinch

is merely a confirmation

but before we reach it

I have

some congruous fruit

reduced to

spirits

which go straight

to De Quincey

who at last

perfects his influence

on vintage growth

mauve

absolution

repairs

worn

fortifications

dates

reshuffle

for those who

can survive six months

in an old-fashioned carrot cake

Fräulein cannot bake

the sad skinhead

is obsessed with the Brontës

Anne hated too much light

Charlotte

was almost dark

and Emily

sculpted grotesque candles

one green one

had obviously been

smoking

the stray butts

asked a dog whether

proper extroverts

irritate the nostrils

or ears

the smell

of music

from behind

the spheres

strikes us as ordinary

Captain Zoom

occasionally rises

when his chair is

sent to photograph

birds

like other men

his work is never

on the shelves at home

in his own words

no one tends

to hurt anyone but himself

with a pencil

orange tips and

red admirals spot

paintbrushes

with their antennae and powder

the egg with the

radio

sweeps for tea and toast

along the Thames

it knows

that a cup is looking

to procure some

boiling water

for its friends

SUPERFLUOUS RUSSET LABELS

Brassy fragments of the dance below reached us

      orange functions like a balcony

because of an allergy to chocolate

      Naylor trod on a tomato

to create a globular, jarlike form

        Slightly crimson around the cheekbones

I began to imagine that I was a rustic bridge

          Light and shade created by Arthur Acton

Let John, the Baptist, rejoice with the Salmon—

Her face was still tan from living in Santa Barbara

      mahogany paintbox

Thomson's sea-pen (below) is related to coral

for as water quencheth a flaming fire

   The Masai were ticklish but potentially profitable

   strange as reindeer with their orange glow

       With locks sparckled abroad, and rosie Coronet

Perkin Warbeck was really the Duke of York

        making a false set of teeth out of an orange skin

corpulent (copper)

        much khaki

white gold kills red

      Yet if Artaud's therapists had known

Crabs haven't quite caught on; perhaps they refuse to. The idea that they are genial supports is merely a stagy tableau. A stone crab no one sees has rotated. It fills a major gap. A team of scientists on a remote island must find a way to stop gigantic mutant crabs (with human-type eyes rather than stalked ones) from reproducing and invading the world's oceans. Enormous birds and bees encourage the scientists to compete. Jules Verne enters. Roger Corman works on his blood. The thoroughly evil Dr Bang unscrews his artificial arm and releases his 'peeler'. Made of H-bombs and twine, it is universally disliked. The ubiquitous phantom crab lives in the catacombs of the opera house. The ghost crab billows to attract mates. These pods join in. As a crab swims sideways, it clicks or snaps a fake pod onto the inner surface of a joint to optimize lift.

The black tips of large pens make me sick, but most crabs are chilled, packed into Styrofoam boxes, with a supply of pots for recreational use. Evidence suggests that settlers wore simple crabs to protect their feet. Crabs in an area without grass can beef up a dull scene. Initially pink, Van Gogh turned red as he yelled at his sponge. Then he cut off a piece of algae. Rembrandt moved a crab with his van. Some painters operate from a skipjack boat, draping a roller over the side, but most people decorate crabs casually, on a plate or at the beach. Virginia was one of the first wives to be considered aquatic because she snorkeled after meals.

The miserly Eugene Krabs will do almost anything for profit. He quietly goes about his business—slathering sunscreen on sections of drain pipe—as if you weren't there. Sebastian the crab has released two reggae albums for children. He plays organ, piano and clavinet, and is one of the only instrumentalists on the crustacean music scene. Already in great demand, he is also available as a beanbag. Crabs in the air vent as they go by. On clear nights, English crabs can see the moon reflected in a beer can. The moon beats and flaps, causing the tides.

The Plankton Mimic is both fascinating and likable. When he drifts into a pet store, normally docile crabs yodel and cavort until the whole store is in an uproar. Aristophanes co-authored the multi-volume *Ten Legs? No Way!* In Greek mythology, the helmet crab was rewarded with a skateboard after mocking the special pleading of the evolutionists. Rudyard Kipling is said to have liked his crabs 'just so'. Jorge, a fry cook, is hard to know. He may be damaged in the process of grasping a potato. He responds to changes in mayo.

I like to think that a crab's apron can be pulled back to reveal an area in the rear where work is easier to do with your hands than with any implement provided. Some people get crabs on the lips and face. It's no wonder that fancy restaurants provide napkins and wet wipes for customers who are lucky enough to have developed the habit of eating before they become weak and lethargic and eventually die. A box crab physically smothered the research bug. Frozen crabs are OK. This brilliant reddish-orange crab is actually Will Ferrell. Junkies steal crabs. Menus float. Crab art is feasible but difficult because, aside from mosaics on aquarium floors, crab images don't like to get wet. Carol Ormes of Crabworks has the best time in my apartment. The secret of success, says a fisherman who was caught in the 1940s, is to go overboard in a hot air balloon.